THE METTLE
NETTLES

Copyright © 2015 Marian Conway, Green Gate Farm

All rights reserved. No part of this publication may be transmitted or reproduced without written permission from the copyright holder or the Publisher.

This book is a source of information only and not a medical book. It is advised that no herb should be used without first consulting a doctor or qualified medical herbalist.

The author or the publisher cannot be held responsible for any adverse reactions to the use of any herb or derivative in this book.

ISBN: 978-1-910044-06-3

Published by Shanway Press,1-3 Eia Street, Belfast, BT14 6BT   www.shanway.com

Cover design: Emma Heddles

Dear Reader,

Are you one of those people who never lost their sense of awe?

I can stand gazing in wonderment at sprouting wheatgrass or a cheeky Orange Tip butterfly happily nibbling away at a nettle leaf.

Yet, many times during the past few years something occurred which has left me totally dumbstruck.

It began when I was attending the wake of a dear elderly neighbour. I was chatting to two delightful ladies when, as is usual while I'm in company, the conversation turned to folklore, nature and gardening among other things. These two ladies were literally begging me to tell them all about my nettle therapy.

I usually neither notice nor care what people wear, but I was suddenly struck by the irony of these two lovely ladies adorned with expensive jewellery and their vast knowledge of detox (and botox) desperate for more details about my humble nettle therapy, as I sat there in my £7 jacket and denim jeans.

An elderly, amiable gentleman sitting nearby had now joined in our lively conversation and he insisted that I immediately (yes, right there and then) write down for him, in detail, my 'recipe' (as he called it) for thinning hair!

To our immense credit, we have progressed materially, but although we don't (I haven't been elected to speak for others but I certainly don't) want to return to the so-called 'good-old-days' with no central heating and cold, damp houses, there is a hunger and a thirst for the simple decent things in life. Nowadays people have material prosperity yet many are dying of loneliness. Nettles ignite the spark that reminds us of innocent, childhood simplicity as we played on wonderful, carefree summer days where being 'busy' meant running through fields, ditches and *sheughs*.

I believe we are put on this earth to help others and if this book makes you feel good then I am privileged to share it with you.

This book is dedicated in honour of St Fiachra, the patron saint of gardeners.

Bless you, dear reader and my sincere prayer is that you may grow in health and dazzle with happiness as you embark on this wondrous adventure of learning and growing.

Marian

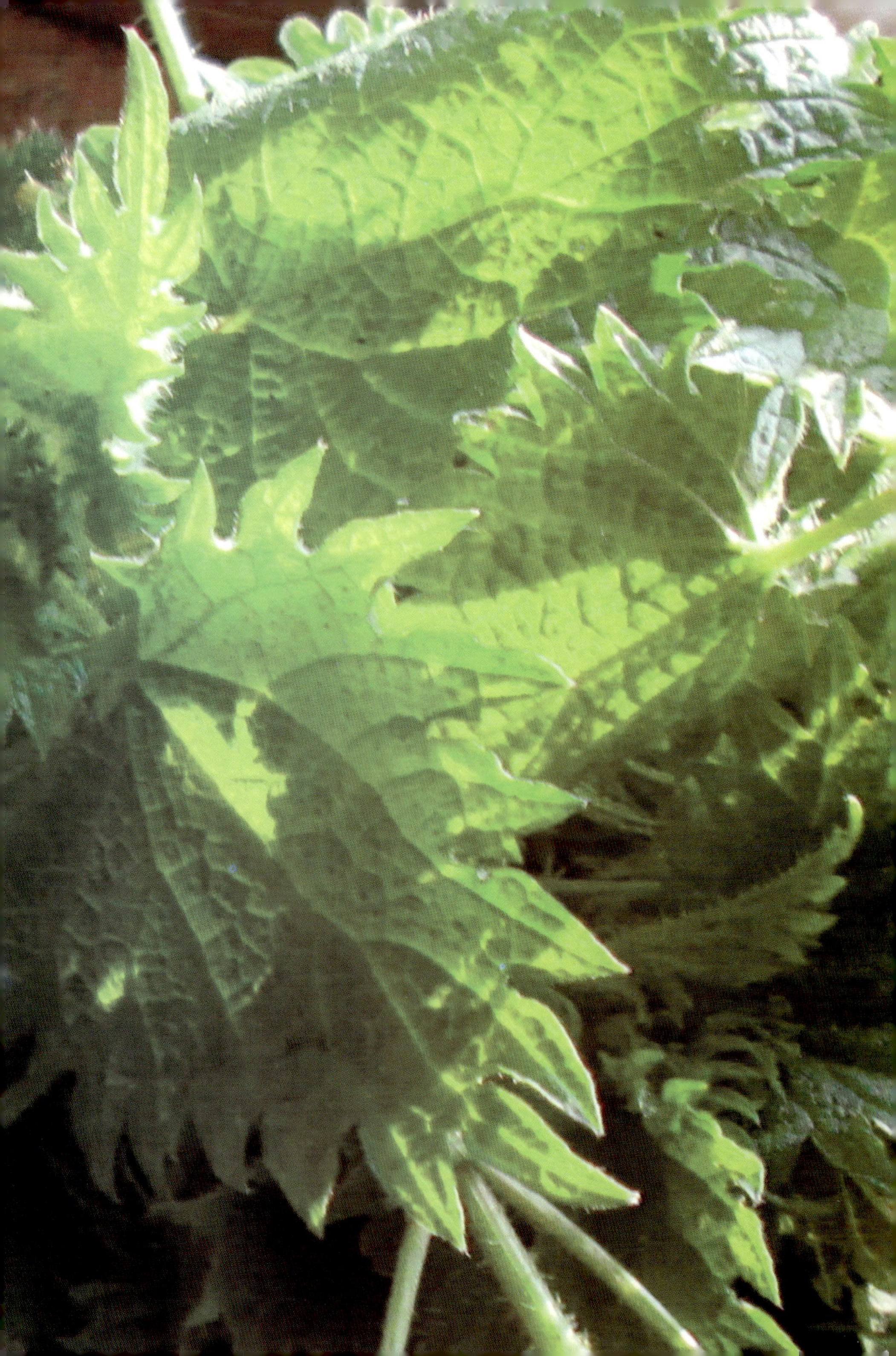

CHAPTER ONE

Nettle - It's only natural

"I can't wait until I get home this evening to tell my missus what I've seen you doing this day" exclaimed Mick who was one of the builders carrying out renovation work on our home.

That morning Mick had watched me dander down to the bottom of our field and gather a bag full of young, spring nettles. Mick now gazed in incomprehension as I simmered the nettles in a saucepan of boiling water.

I really like to analyse the various expressions on people's faces when they first watch me prepare my nettle therapy. Mick's face was a picture as he stared at the nettle stems protruding from underneath the saucepan lid and he gave a hearty laugh, in itself a tonic.

I was reminded of one spectator who remarked with indignation: "Surely no civilised person either eats or drinks nettles."

I always thoroughly enjoy being in the company of elderly people.
They are a vast wealth of folklore, history, wisdom and craic because they have been there, done it and learned from years of experience.

Whenever I mention my much loved herbs (can you believe even plants thrive better on love!) to the elderly, my heart jumps for joy as their faces illuminate with the awareness of nature's fascinating secrets. They have worked on, lived off and respected the land and are well-versed in the uniqueness, myths, superstition, energies and healing powers of trees, shrubs, plants and flowers growing in the living, sacred earth.

I cared for my beloved, elderly parents, until they died, here, in the home place.
I loved every minute of those precious years. They cared for us when we were children and I consider it a blessed privilege to have looked after them when the roles were reversed.

I honestly admit my one regret is that I did not listen more intently to them. Sure, I listened but with one ear because you can't put an oul head on young shoulders and, being a teenager, I was more interested in pop music than which 'weed' helps flatulence. I mistakenly assumed I would always hear that yarn repeated some other time, not realising just how little time there really was.

When you are at home and in harmony with nature you are at home and in harmony with God.

My wonderful wise and sensible father maintained that "herbs such as red clover (Trifolium pratense) and hyssop – (Hyssopus officinalis) – hyssop derives from Hebrew name Esob and (please note hyssop should not be used by Epileptics) are mentioned in the Bible because in our hedges and fields there's an 'erb for every sickness."
(In Irish this is *Ta luibh ar gach leighas*).

My father, like many if his generation, had familiarised himself with the elements and bonded with the land that he so passionately loved.

He inhaled the aroma of the soil beneath his fingernails and he intuitively understood how to commune with the plants' energies. We spent many happy hours discussing how God, in His guidance, provided plants that looked similar to the body parts or organs which they healed. Hawthorn – Quickthorn, Skeaghbush – (Crataegus oxyacantha) leaves resemble your heart while the veins on Ribwort Plantain – Rat's tail – (Plantago lanceolata) are similar to your ribs. Nowadays I joyfully reminisce with our children about the lively discussions we used to have concerning Airmeith.

Saint Fiachra (Fiachrach, Fiacre) who was born in Ireland and died on August 18, 670AD is the Patron Saint of gardeners, florists and cab drivers. However there is no Patron Saint of herbs although there is a Patroness of herbalism and her name is Airmeith.

Airmeith lived with her two brothers, one of whom was called Miach and her father Dian Cecht (or Dian Ceacht) who was a Doctor and a Druid, in Co. Sligo in 485BC.
They tended the Tuatha De Danann soldiers during the Battle of Moytirra.

Nuadhu, the De Danaan chieftain, had his hand cut off and Miach embalmed it then successfully reattached it. In a fit of jealously Dian Cecht murdered his son Miach. As Miach lay in his grave at Tara, his grieving sister Airmeith noticed that 365 herbs grew from different parts of his body. She realised that each herb protruded from the body part it could heal. As Airmeith retrieved all the herbs, she knew that from then on her mission would be to teach people about herbs. She began documenting which ailment each herb cured. In a rage, Nuadha tossed the herbs in the air where a heavy gust of wind scattered them all over every forest, wood, glen, field and hedge throughout Ireland, where they still grow today.

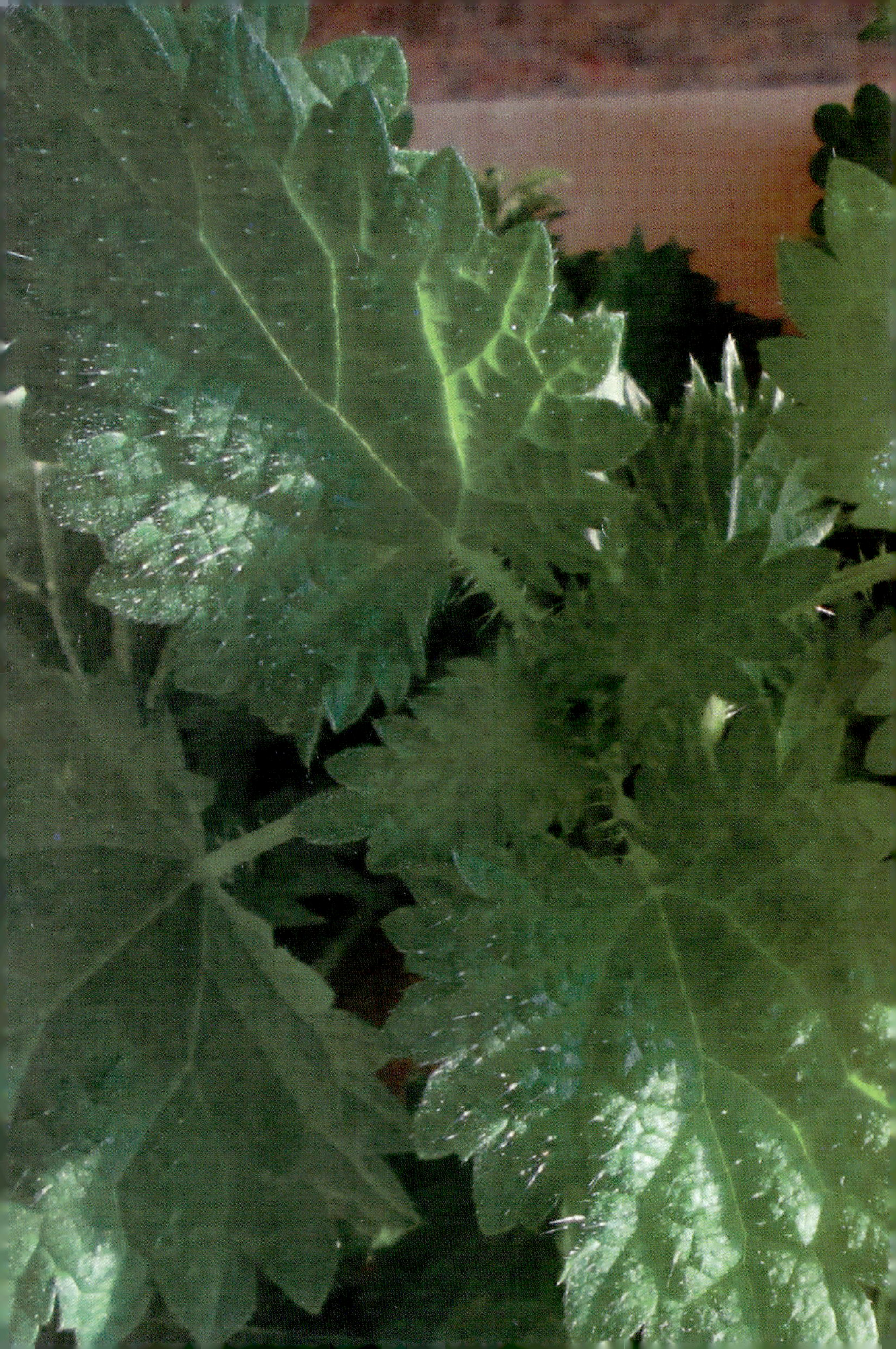

CHAPTER TWO

From human doing to the magic of human being

Modern life, with its brilliant and admirable advancements in technology and medicine, has eradicated our interaction with plants and nature. We are so constantly stressed with busyness that we simply haven't the time to talk to a plant or hug a tree. In our constant quest for the outer remedy we want (not need) the quick fix and we want (not need) it now. But, just as nature intended, herbs with their gentle healing, body regulators, do not provide quick fixes.

Some people have been brainwashed into believing that if something is sophisticated and cost a lot of money then surely it must be good. Others are suspicious of anything that is simple and straightforward. They can not even begin to contemplate how a free 'weed' growing wild in a field could be useful for anything, yet alone be beneficial to a specific ailment or disease.

A wee bit of common sense...
I am not, and do not intend to become, either a doctor of orthodox medicine or a herbalist. I have a lot of reverence for both professions.

Immediately you suspect any ailment, it is vital to get a doctor's diagnosis and advice. Herbs are powerful living nature beings and where they are concerned ignorance is definitely not bliss. Only an idiot would self-diagnose or even consider using any herb medicinally without first consulting a doctor.

Never use any herb medicinally, or for culinary purposes, without first being positive of its identification.

Unless in the hands of a qualified herbalist all herbs may not be safe, as some herbs cannot be used for certain ailments or can interact with pharmaceutical medicines, while other herbs have many uses. So have a wee bit of common sense: Don't be a fool, ignorance is not cool.

Simply be with nature beings and relearn your sense of awe. I have a deep respect, love and compassion for all living beings on our earth. Each creature has his or her own job to do. My children enjoy watching me gardening because when I dig up a worm, I pat him gently, bless him and return him to his ploughing, as I thank God and nature for such healthy, fertile soil.

Human beings who simply be with nature are never alone as each plant or herb is alive. When you open your senses to the nature being within each stone or every blade of grass and relearn your sense of awe – this is a powerful tonic in itself. When you relate to a plant or herb's nature being, you have taken one step away from the desperate helplessness, hopelessness and sheer loneliness of illness where all you could envisage was no way. You are taking one step towards a ripening of your heart and a healing wholeness of your body.

You relate to a plant or a herb being the same way you relate to a human being. You simply be with them. In my experience it is best to harmonise with one plant or herb at a time.

Choose a plant that you fancy then gaze at its colours, its shape and its curves or lines. Feel the texture of its petals, stems, leaves, berries, thorns or veins. Send it a beam of white light. Imagine you have swapped bodies so you are now the plant and it is you. Be not separate, be as one. Talk to it and listen to it speak to your heart. How do you feel about each other?

Ask it to help make you whole.

This way you develop a connection with the plants spirit and you gain a heightened understanding of your own spirit. Years ago I learned a truly enriching exercise, which I practice daily after I say the Our Father, a powerful prayer in which the word I is not said.

Inwardly say 'bless you' to every person, animal, creature, plant or thing whom you see. Say 'bless you' to yourself, when you look in the mirror. When you practise saying 'bless you' (even to whoever or whatever irritates you) the results will be amazing and you will experience a miracle each day.

You are blessed with many magical, light moments in your life.
I also realise that even when the sky is at its blackest I can still clearly see starlight. The reason I have devoted this entire book to nettles is because many moons ago during a particularly sad time in my life, following the death of my dear father, I experienced a magical light moment.

For years I had been interested in the secret lives of plants, but now I felt drawn to the culinary, cosmetic and therapeutic benefits of nettles. So began a fascinating relationship of respect, love, joy, banter and plenty of craic as nature beings guided me into their living, mysterious, sacred ways.

Stand on top of a hill on a windy day and cut open a feather pillow. The feathers will scatter, making it impossible to gather them all up. This is what happens when you gossip and attempt to ruin someone's reputation, as it is impossible to ever retrieve all the damage done.

Unfortunately, and unfairly, nettles have gained a notoriously bad reputation over the years. They are reviled as pests by gardeners and if you've accidentally brushed against a bunch as you played on wonderful summer days, you'll soon learn the painful consequences of being 'nipped by nettles'. People even associate nettles with anything irritating such as 'he felt nettled' or 'why do you nettle her?' In 1733 an English author, the Reverend T Silvester referred to nettles as 'ignoble weeds'.

Shakespeare disliked nettles and included them in mad king Lear's wreath.
In Achill in Co Mayo it was traditionally said that an ill-tempered person must have pissed on nettles. People also regard nettles as a sign of neglect or desolation. Recently, I was visiting a graveyard when I overheard two ladies ridicule a family in the parish who were supposedly not caring for their parents grave because it had nettles growing alongside the surround.

However, nettles were held in high esteem by our ancestors and I believe it is about time our nettle friends were restored to their former glory.

The German painter and mathematician Albrecht Duerer (1471-1528) shows an angel clasping stinging nettles in his hands flying into Heaven.

Nettle; *Neantog* which belongs to the Urticaceae famliy, ***neanntoga*** young cooked nettle, ***neannta loiscneach*** older tougher nettle – which is ruled by planet Mars, has the zodiac sign Scorpio and which is commonly referred to in Ulster as Cul Faiche or field cabbage.

CHAPTER THREE

Back to our roots

It's a quare good job for the sake of our relatively innocent wee nettle family *(Urticaceae)* here in Ireland and in Britain, that some of the nastier species of nettles live abroad.

Urtica heterophyilia and Urtica crenulato in East India, can produce symptoms similar to lockjaw while Indonesia's Urtica urentissima can be fatal. With friends like that, our nettles, the critters, don't need enemies.

You'll probably laugh your head off when I say this, but by the time you've read this book and, hopefully, practised some of the nettle therapy, you'll regard dame nettle as your new best friend – honestly!

There are plants in Ireland and Britain which are called Nettles, but which belong to the mint (labiatae or lamiaceae) family.

There is white dead-nettle, lamium album (lamium is derived from the Greek word laimos, meaning throat) which is also called blind nettle, deaf nettle, dumb nettle and dead nettle because of its inability to sting. Far from being dead this very-much-alive-and-well hairy perennial plant grows amongst stinging nettles and because it has leaves similar to stinging nettles, grazing animals think it stings so they don't eat it. However, once its big, white, bee-shaped hooded flowers appear there is no resemblance to the stinging nettle flowers.

This intelligent plant then deals with this new survival problem by making its flowers smell and taste nasty. Its common name is bee nettle and it safeguards its nectar for the bees alone by forming a barricade of fine hairs just above the nectar, thus preventing tiny, thieving insects from entering. Then when the bees arrive with the precious pollen they and they alone are rewarded with the nectar.

Earlier in the year white dead-nettle and red dead-nettle (Lamium purpureum) or red archangel look alike, but later on the similarity ends when red dead-nettle has lovely, showy, pinkish purple aromatic, nectar laden flowers, which lure bees. When grown in shady or cluttered areas red dead-nettle will be tall with a dull appearance while if grown in sparse areas it will be short and creeping.

Years ago in Co Meath the brewed roots of red dead-nettle were applied to hasten out measles rash.

There's also yellow dead-nettle (Lamiastrum galeobdolon) or yellow archangel whose common name is weasel snout due to its strongly scented hooded yellow flowers, with red strips on the lower lip.

White dead-nettle, red dead-nettle and yellow dead-nettle all share the nickname archangel because they are still in bloom on September 29th (yellow archangel doesn't flower quite as long as white and red) which is the feast day of St Michael the archangel, the protector and comforter we turn to for protection, strength and courage. Sacred, healing plants and herbs have long been included in rituals or religious services and monks work extensively with herbal tinctures, while it was widely believed that the white, red and yellow dead-nettles all offered protection from any evil spirits.

There is also the lovely spotted dead-nettle (Lamium maculatum) which is rare here in the north of Ireland. It grows about 12 inches high, has pinkish purple flowers and each light green leaf has a wee central silver strip. Then there is common hemp nettle (Galeopsis tetrahit) with its pink or lemon flowers and large flowered hemp nettle (Galeopsis speciosa) with pale yellow flowers above a purple lower lip.

Henbit dead-nettle (Lamium amplexicaule) which is the rarest nettle of all blooms from April to August then blooms again during autumn. Although the flowers don't fully open bees are regular visitors.

However in this book we concentrate mainly on forming a relationship with our 2ft high (60cm) annual SMALL NETTLE *Urtica urens* (from latin uro-I burn) whose deeply toothed leaves are light green and whose male and female flowers both grow on one plant. Also our 5ft perennial COMMON STINGING NETTLE *Urtica dioica* (dioica means two houses) whose strongly-toothed leaves are dark green. As you will soon discover there is nothing common about Mr and Mrs stinging nettle, who are also called greater nettle. By late Spring the male and female have similar small greenish flowers growing on separate plants, the difference being that Mr Nettle's flowers grow diagonally facing upright, while Mrs Nettle's flowers curve in tassle-like, catkin clusters. They are dioecious with only male on some plants and only female on others.

To release pollen, Mr Nettle simply flicks it in the air where it lands on Mrs Nettle's flowers.

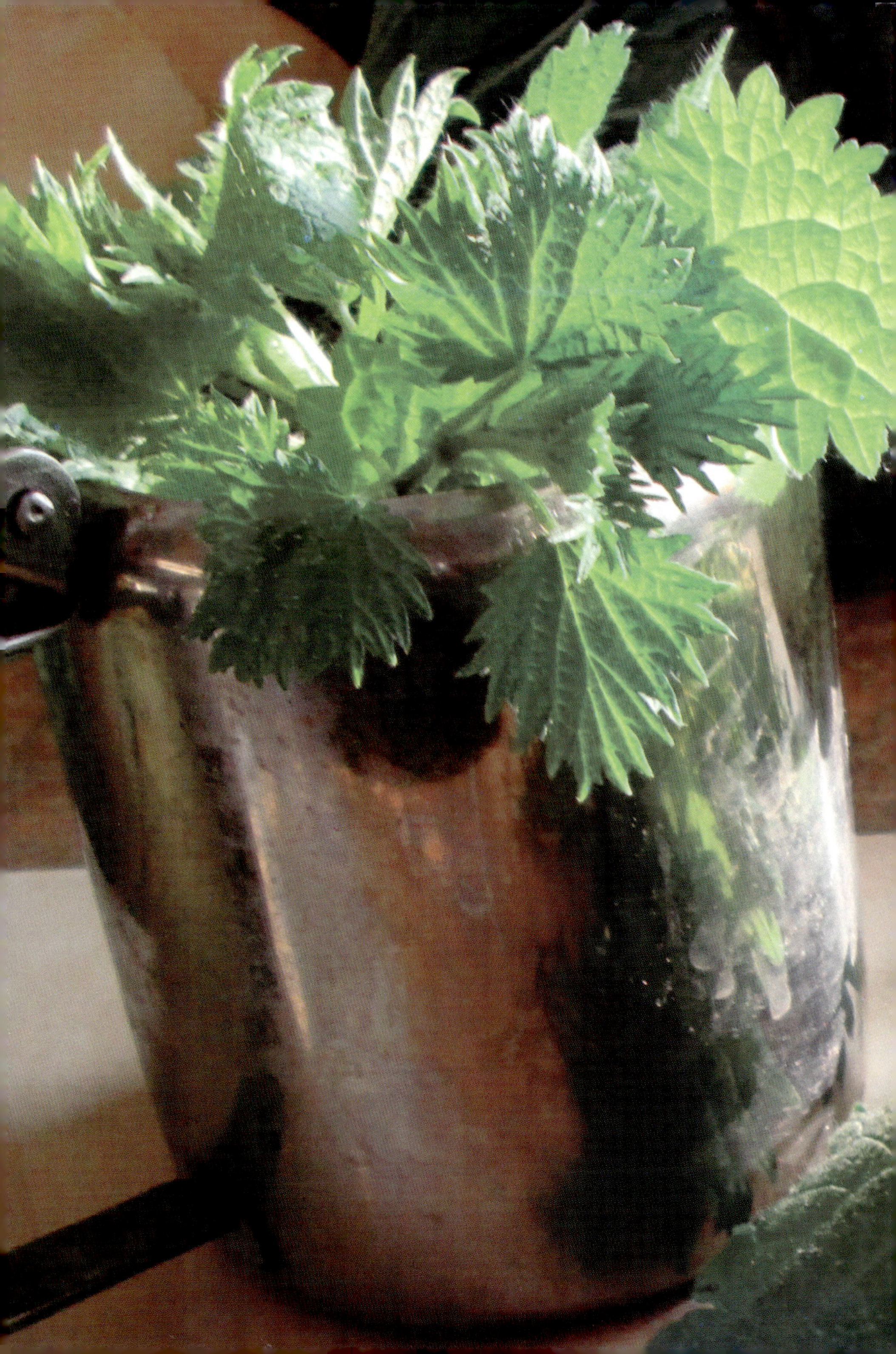

CHAPTER FOUR

Bringing outdoors indoors

Where to gather nettles
Before you go tearing off excitedly nettle gathering please don't think I'm being impertinent when I ask if you can positively identify a nettle?

I'm a country-loving wellington-wearing woman, yet I understand and respect that, for whatever reason, maybe you have never seen a real, live nettle in your life. The Labiatae family's non-stinging fragrant, cat-loving catnip/catmint (Nepeta cataria) looks similar to nettles and even tends to grow beside them. The labiatae family's non-stinging, hedge woundwort (Stachys sylvatica) also has similar leaves to nettles.

So please ensure you can identify a nettle. If in doubt about identity, definitely don't. Most plants are protected by law and uprooting them in the countryside is illegal.

People are usually delighted to get rid of nettles, but please be respectful and courteous by always obtaining specific permission to legally enter anyone's land.

It is of vital importance to ensure that the nettles have not been sprayed with any chemical or chemical fertiliser. It is preferable to avoid nettles growing near dirty polluted waters, or railway lines or roadsides, due to traffic pollution. Try to gather nettles in the countryside or woods and forests, where God in His goodness has allowed the simplicity of nature to reign.

This incredibly simple yet awe-inspiring exercise has to be experienced to be believed. When you breathe in God's fresh air and gather fresh, nutritious nettles, you feel rejuvenated in body, mind and spirit. You are doing something to help yourself.

Each and every time I gather nettles, I learn something about the world, about life, about nature, about tranquility, about helping others and about myself.

One morning I was in our field gathering nettles (and dandelion leaves) accompanied by our cats. When I'm out in God's healthy, fresh air I check if I am holding my breath or shallow breathing into my throat only. I open my mouth and inhale fresh air into my body then exhale. My husband John and our beloved children were happily playing a game of football in our garden.

I looked at my precious family and listened to their magical laughter which echoed the mysterious sounds of nature surrounding us. As I gazed at the magnificent view of Lough Neagh, Slieve Gullion and the Cooley Mountains I thought "This happiness, this joy, this pure simplicity is so priceless that no amount of money could purchase, in any shop, anywhere in the world, what my eyes see now, what my ears hear now and how my spirit soars now".

If for whatever reason, you can't gather nettles yourself, could someone (who knows what a nettle looks like) gather them for you? If this is impossible you can still help yourself by consulting a professional herbalist or reputable health food store or mail order supplier.

Another brilliant idea for those dears who can't travel, is creating a little nettle plot, somewhere near your home – we'll discuss this later on.

Never give up on yourself, or say "what's the point sure there's no way" because there is plenty of point and there is always hope! Please do not say "Och, sure I'm too old" because 60, 70 and 80 is the new 40 and 50. This truly is the era for all the wonderful, full-of-life seniors I see everywhere. All the fun, excitement and sheer joy of being alive should not end just because of a few wrinkles or grey hairs. I am no spring chicken and I have plenty of rusty parts and bits starting to fall off yet each day I am thankful to God for His gift of the sheer joy of being alive.

When to gather nettles
For external use (footbaths etc – we'll discuss this later) nettles can be gathered and used up until September / October.

For internal use, it is of vital importance that nettles are gathered in season, which is from the early spring until the beginning of July. This is because from the first week of July onwards a chemical change occurs in nettles, which forms small crystalline particles in their leaves (*cystoliths*), making them taste bitter, feel gritty and even damaging to your kidneys. Remember: for internal use, in-season only.

What you can do is take advantage of the golden opportunity of gradually gathering nettles during season, then drying and storing them for use during autumn and winter.

How to gather nettles
Rubber gloves are best worn when gathering nettles or if you've pains in your hands wear warm gloves underneath rubber gloves.

Remember Mrs Nettle is soon going to be your new best friend so mind your manners and treat her like a lady. (You even have to wear gloves to touch her)

Don't rip her body out of the soil, thus damaging her roots and eliminating future generations. Wearing gloves just gently snip off upper, young, fresh leaves or use scissors to cut them off. Both Mr and Mrs Nettle enjoy this trimming, which encourages healthy, new growth. When I encounter a huge bunch of nettles I can almost hear their whispers of "please notice me, use me."

Gathering and harvesting nettles
All herbs should be gathered early in the day before their volatile head and body oils are evaporated by the midday sunshine.

On a dry morning, I gather nettles from the bottom of our field once the dew has dried on them, so I prefer not to wash them. If you are concerned about air or human pollutants then rinse them, shake them and lay out thinly on paper towels. As soon as possible tie into small bunches. If you make the bunches big, air can't circulate and they will rot inside.

Hang the bunches upside down (using clothes pegs or hair clasps or paper hooks) in a warm, dry, well-ventilated area such as the roof space, attic or airing cupboard not in a steamy bathroom or kitchen. Never dry in direct sunlight.

My husband, John, showed me another great way to dry nettles on a drying frame, which is simply made by tacking a length of close wire mesh or cloth to a square or rectangular wooden frame made from dismantled, wooden pallets. (John makes all our garden furniture out of discarded, wooden pallets and it's just grand). Keep the nettles apart, not in bunches, and turn them over occasionally to allow air to circular between all the leaves.

In about five to six weeks (maybe longer) when the nettles are completely dry, they will be crispy, brittle and ready for autumn/winter storage. They are also still alive and can sting. Your rooms may smell nice and homely but once dried, nettles will lose a lot of their flavour and energies if not stored immediately. The best containers are brown or green glass-lidded jars which deflect light – but clear glass will do – or you can use dry paper bags which must be kept dry but do avoid metal or plastic jars. Be sure to label and date all jars.

Gather your precious nettles daily during season and you will gradually store-up enough for one autumn/winter only, as God will supply your garden with another fresh crop for you to gather and harvest next year.

Harvesting nettle roots
If you want to harvest nettle roots for external use during winter (we'll discuss hair tincture, baths etc. later on) dig or pull up the nettle roots very early in the day or late in the evening, during spring or summer but preferably during autumn, when they are at their most potent and when you can still find them before they die away. Clean with a cloth or disused, soft nailbrush. Larger roots can be cut, before drying on your drying frame.

Proverb: 1753 'nettle's lesson'
Tender-handed stroke a nettle

And it stings you for your pains;
Grasp it like a man of mettle,
And it soft as silk remains

Naughty nettles
The Anglo-Saxon name for nettle is netel – from *noedl* meaning needle, referring to the notorious small hairs within the nettle leaves, whose irritating stings have caused nettles to be shunned as outcasts by society.

The mechanism of the sting resembles that of the hypodermic needle, yet nettles pre-date the syringe by centuries.

Each silica-formed firm hair has a fragile tip which, even if gently touched, will snap off, baring a pinnacle which contains and expresses into the skin, formic acid and histamine, held in cells within the base, (which are destroyed during cooking).

Even if you smell nettles too close, as I constantly enjoy doing, they will sting your nose and that is probably why, in Ireland, nettles are nicknamed 'fire heat' or *'Teine faid'*
Did you know that the nettle was the most stunning flower in the whole of the Garden of Eden but once the snake had tempted Eve it crouched underneath the nettle and from that day onwards the nettle would sting.

Hair of the dog
Tradition goes that if bitten by a dog, a hair of the same dog placed on the wound hastens healing. (Also, believe it or not, the best remedy for nappy rash is the child's own urine rubbed on the affected area)

Likewise, the best antidote for burning, itchy, yet benign nettle rash (urticaria) is fresh nettle juice, taken from the broken stem and rubbed on the spot.
An infusion of either basil, chamomile, rosemary or thyme applied to the rash will give you cool relief. Another remedy is to rub the rash with either sage, rosemary, plantain or mint leaves.

My husband John maintains that the quickest remedy for nettle sting is to rub on the juice of houseleek (Sempervivum).

A neighbouring farmer told me he keeps a tube of toothpaste in his shed to rub on nettle stings. However, the simplest cure of all which, coincidently, usually grows quite close to nettles is the Broad-leaved Dock (Rumex obtusifolius) that is usually called docken in Ireland and whose neutralising chemicals give soothing relief.

Here in Ireland the cure is hastened by first spitting on the docken leaf then as you rub the rash keep repeating the following charm:

A nettle stung me, docken cured me.
Irish – *Neantog a dhoig me copog leighis me.*

Or the commonly used ancient rhyme;
nettle out, dock in, dock remove the nettle sting.

Remember; you can always rub a dab of your own urine on the sting.

CHAPTER FIVE

Gentleness from the strong

When faced with a challenge, we are advised to grasp the nettle. I believe that nettles are gentle beings who show us that the more respectful, loving, gentle and considerate we are towards all forms of life on this earth, the stronger we become. To grasp the strong yet gentle nettle shows us that although we all make mistakes and get stung by the consequences, mistakes do not make us any particular thing. They are life lessons to help us learn and grow.

When we were learning to walk, each time we fell down, we did not stay down, but, determined to do it, got up and tried again and again. The staying power of nettles has shown me how to grasp the nettle, go for it, keep going, keep trying, never lose sight of your goal and always have a dream.

I also believe nettles to be so absolutely valuable, in their usefulness and versatility, that if they didn't sting they would all be gobbled up by browsing, hungry animals so us humans and up to 40 species of insect would lose out. The lovely diachrysia chrysitis moth and our beautiful butterflies Red Admiral, Peacock, Painted Lady and Small Tortoiseshell lay their eggs on stinging nettles and then the resulting caterpillars feast on the nettle leaves.

Nettles are the winter home of aphids who produce honeydew which ants eat. These aphids hang around young spring nettles and are then eaten by woodland birds and our valuable slug-eating ladybirds. These crafty creatures know how to manoeuvre through the hairs without getting stung.

During late summer, birds devour the massive pile of seeds produced by nettles. There is a traditional Irish saying: 'Every man that was ever born and bred, and the corncrake truly loves the nettle.' Nettles provide early cover for the lovely corncrake, with its distinctive call, to lay its eggs. Unfortunately this fascinating bird became extinct here in the north of Ireland around 20 years ago although it can still be heard in other parts of Ireland. Evidently, nettles perform a vital role in helping the survival of our precious wildlife.

Negative nettle
It is hard to believe there is anything negative about our wonderful nettle but nettles, being high in potassium, are diuretic (you will form and pass more urine) so avoid with other diuretics. Nettles are also a uterine stimulant so if you are pregnant it is important to not take nettles internally without first consulting your doctor or a qualified herbalist. The upper side of the nettle leaf contains the stings so many folk eat 'raw' uncooked nettle leaves by picking from underneath, folding them lengthways until the upper side is covered, squeezing them tightly by hand to cut the spines and then chewing. But please be careful as eating uncooked nettles can produce unpleasant symptoms. Nettles can also lower blood sugar so if you are on medication check with a qualified herbalist.

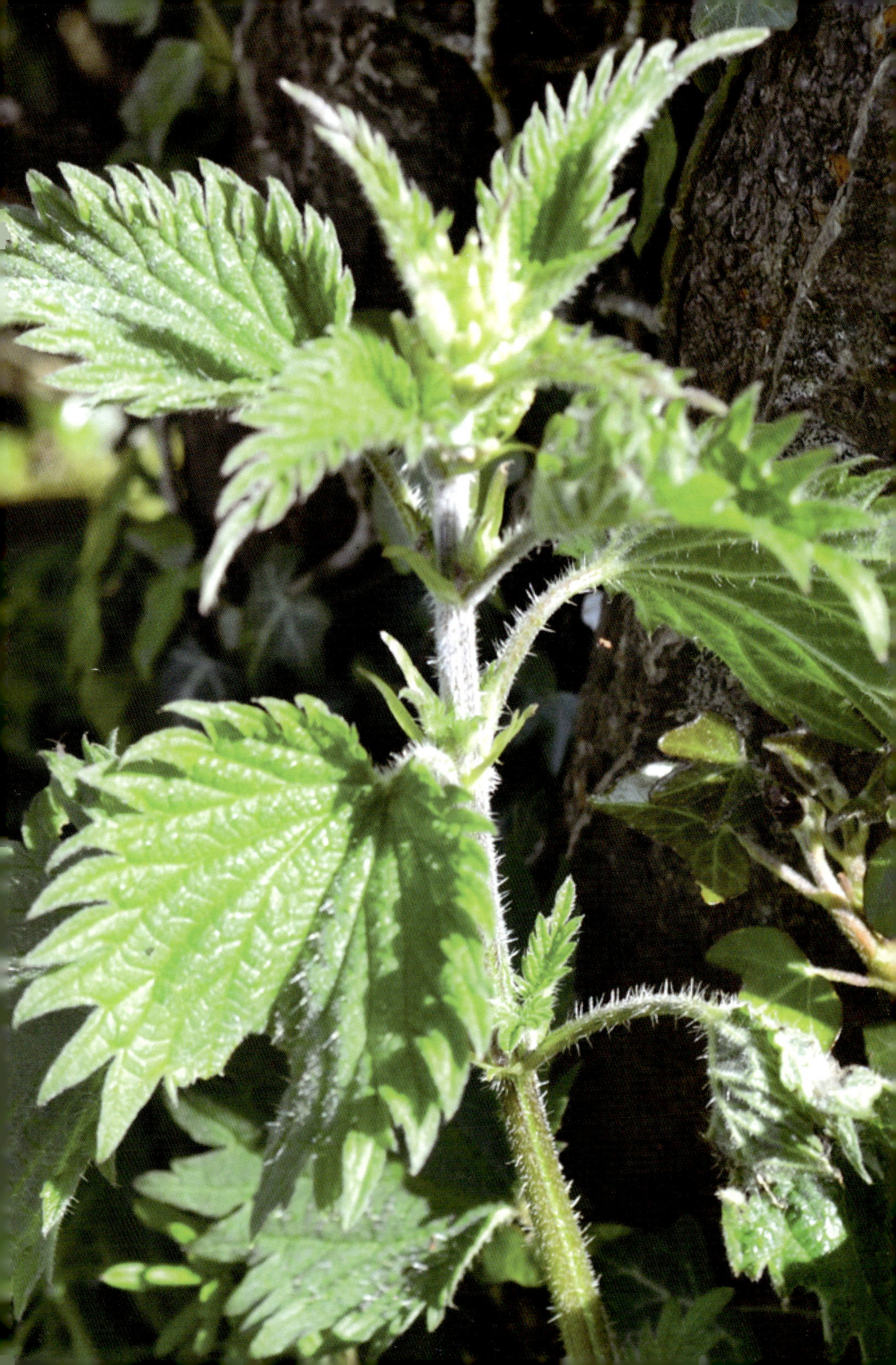

CHAPTER SIX

For food and drink

Stinging Nettle – Spring tonic tea
Nutritious nettles are high in vitamins A and C plus minerals iron, potassium and calcium, and also silica.

Saint Kevin is supposed to have survived for seven years on a diet of only sorrel and nettles.

For centuries our native nettles have been used as medicinal food and although nettles are not going to make you 16 again my nourishing and revitalising Stinging Nettle Spring tonic tea will go a long way towards making you feel 16 in mind, body, spirit and soul. In the traditional Irish ballad where the old woman was plucking young nettles it was possibly for a cup of tay (tea).

Every time I mention my Stinging Nettle Spring tonic tea to someone to someone whether I'm on a walk or at a wake, they implore me to tell them more. P.S. As I've mentioned the word walk I can't resist asking if you know that it is almost impossible to argue with someone when walking together?

Some people have told me that they used to spend a small fortune on expensive detox tablets, until I explained to them how nettles gently stimulate the liver and kidneys; rid the body of excess uric acid, winter phlegm and accumulated toxins; purify as well as strengthen the blood and are an excellent (and cheap) aid to spring detox your system and revitalise your body.

If you have any allergy, such as annual uninvited hayfever, drink up to three mugfuls of Stinging Nettle Spring tonic tea daily. You can buy nettle tea in shops but the freshly gathered (free) nettles are naturally much more beneficial.

I am, and always have been, an early riser (thank God to be able to get out of bed) so each morning, for about five weeks, during spring, when the stinging nettle is in season (as discussed earlier) I make enough fresh nettle tea to last one day.

Gather a small handful of young stinging nettle tops. Put the nettles tops in a non aliminium teapot (not the one you normally make tea in) or a non aluminium saucepan. Pour on boiling water but do not boil as boiling destroys most of their medicinal properties. Infuse for five to 10 minutes. You'll adore the aroma, which fills your kitchen.

About 30 minutes before breakfast, sip, do not gulp, one mugful of the tea. Gradually, throughout the day, sip two more mugfuls. You can add a slice of ginger root or a sprig of mint or peppermint or chamomile or lemon balm or a dash of lemon juice to taste, if you wish.

You could add a few bitter dandelion leaves - *leontodon taraxacum* (Irish: caisearbhan). Give any leftover tea to your houseplants and you'll soon reap the benefits.
Please don't be so enthusiastic that you drink nettle tea day and night. As we've already discussed herbs are not a quick fix but prefer to work slowly but surely.

It is never safe to overdo any herb, even our precious nettle, who in my eyes can do no wrong, in the majority of cases.

Chilblains
Rub nettle tea on the affected area.

Sunburn
Dab cool nettle tea on sunburn.

Gout
Do not use nettle tincture (which contains alcohol) for gout. Instead, soak a piece of cloth in a cup of stinging nettle tea and apply to the painful joint.

Nursing mothers
With its high iron content, nettle tea will help stimulate milk production in nursing mothers.

Saint Columba's Broth
In Ireland from the Sixth Century up until around 1900, Saint Columba's Broth or *Brotchan Neantog* was quite a popular meal.

Place a few handfuls of nettle tops in a pan with just enough water to wet the leaves. Simmer for five minutes, strain, add a knob of butter and a little salt. Mash all together and keep turning for five minutes until it is a puree. Slowly add milk, water, fine oatmeal and continue stirring until the mixture thickens.

Simple nettle soup – serves six
The key to this soup is good stock...
225g nettles
160g potatoes
600ml milk
600ml good vegetable or chicken stock
110g onion, chopped
25g butter
Salt and pepper

Peel and chop potatoes. In a saucepan melt butter. Add onion, potatoes, salt and pepper. Put lid on saucepan and simmer gently 15 minutes, stirring occasionally. Add stock, milk, bring to the boil and simmer until potatoes cooked. Mix in nettles and with lid off simmer for 3 minutes. Liquidise then serve.

Nettle soup
5 to 6 large handfuls nettle tops
2 chopped potatoes
1 chopped onion
3 chopped garlic cloves or 6 chopped wild garlic leaves
2 pints of water
a little oil or butter

Put potatoes and onion in a saucepan. Saute in oil or butter. Add nettles, garlic, water and cook for 30 minutes. Season with sea salt and black pepper then serve.

Nettle soup – thick
6 to 8 handfuls chopped nettle tops
a few chopped dandelion leaves
3 pints stock
¼ pint cream
3oz oats
2 leeks or 2 onions
2oz butter
1 egg yolk, beaten
salt, pepper and a pinch of grated nutmeg

Melt the butter and lightly fry onions. Add nettles, oats, stock, salt, pepper and nutmeg. Simmer for approximately 45 minutes.
Cool slightly then stir in cream and egg.
Reheat slowly without boiling then serve

Nettle soup – slight variation on above
1lb nettles
4 potatoes – sliced
1 onion – sliced
½ pint milk
1 pint stock
Salt and pepper
1 tbsp yogurt or the cream from top of the milk

Put the nettles, potatoes, onion, stock, salt and pepper in a saucepan and simmer for 45 minutes. Press the soup through a sieve then back to the saucepan. Slowly add the milk and bring to near boiling. Slowly stir in the yogurt or cream from the top of the milk then serve.

Creamed nettle soup
1lb chopped nettles
4 cupfuls stock – chicken
3 cups thick cream
1 cup finely chopped onion
3 tablespoons butter
Salt and pepper to taste

Melt the butter in a saucepan then add the onion and sauté for a few minutes until light brown. Slowly add the cream and stock then bring to the boil. Add the nettles and return to the boil for a few minutes. Blend all in the mixer, add salt, pepper, reheat if desired then serve this tasty, healthy soup.

Nettled tomato soup
5 handfuls or 1 bowlful nettles
1½ pints meat stock
2 or 3 onions
2lbs tomatoes, skinned and sliced
1 glass white wine
Few parsley leaves finely chopped
1 knob butter for frying
Salt and pepper
A little cream for serving

Put butter and onions in a saucepan and sauté until golden. Add nettles and simmer until tender. Stir in stock and simmer 15 minutes. Put through blender then return to saucepan. Stir in salt, pepper, tomatoes, white wine and parsley. Bring to the boil. Add cream before serving.

Nettled mushroom pie
900g nettles
225g mushrooms sliced
100g breadcrumbs
50g cheese, grated
50g nuts, finely chopped
2 or 3 garlic cloves, crushed
300ml white sauce
1 tablespoon olive oil
1 tablespoon melted butter
Pinch of salt, pepper and nutmeg

Simmer nettles in a little water for 10 minutes.
Drain off water and set nettles aside. Warm olive oil in a saucepan.
Add mushrooms and cook for 10 minutes. Cool for one minute.
Add nettles, white sauce, salt, pepper and nutmeg. Put into a pie dish.
In a separate container mix together breadcrumbs, cheese, nuts and garlic.
Spread over the nettled mushrooms and pour melted butter over the top.
Put into an oven preheated to 190c and leave for 45 minutes.

Nettle Champ – staimpi, thump, cally, ceaile
2lbs peeled potatoes.
1 handful or cupful chopped spring nettle tops
½ pint milk
2oz butter
salt and pepper

Boil the potatoes until soft and while they are boiling simmer the spring nettle tops in the milk for approximately 15 minutes. Drain the potatoes then add the nettles, milk, butter, salt, pepper. Mix well and serve hot – delicious – especially if you make a wee well in the middle and drop in a knob of butter.

Nettle Fritters
5-6 handfuls of nettles
2 eggs, beaten
1 handful flour
salt, pepper and pinch grated nutmeg

Blanch nettles in boiling water for a few minutes. Strain off liquid and dry nettles in a towel. Cut up the nettles then add to the eggs with salt, pepper and nutmeg.
Shape into fritters, roll them in flour then lightly fry on both sides in melted butter.

Nettle sauce/pesto
This makes two full jam pots (or half each amount for one pot) and keeps in the fridge for a few months. It is tasty with spuds, pasta or barbecued meat.
50g chopped nettle leaves.
50g pine kernels.
50g cheese (parmesan, grated).
4 mashed garlic cloves.
150ml olive oil.
Pinch salt.

Puree together the nettles, kernels, cheese and garlic. Stir in the olive oil and salt. Pour into the two jam pots. On top of each pot of sauce pour just under ½ inch olive oil then put in fridge.

Nettle and potato bap
1lb nettle leaves (10 cupfuls) chopped
1lb potatoes peeled and shredded
5oz soft cheese sliced
1 tablespoon olive oil
1 clove garlic sliced
salt and pepper

Simmer the nettle leaves in boiling water for a few minutes, strain then add the garlic, salt and pepper. Heat the olive oil in a lidded pan. Slowly spoon in half the potatoes, half the nettles, all the cheese, the remainder of the nettles and the potatoes. Put the lid on the pan and cook for about 10 minutes on low heat. Turn the bap over and cook for another 15 minutes then serve.

Nettled Sweet Potato Mash
1lb sweet potatoes
225g nettles
1 red onion sliced
150g green peas
3 tablespoons olive oil
salt and pepper

Boil the sweet potatoes, peel, mash and leave aside. Simmer nettles in boiling water for a few minutes, drain off water and chop. Heat oil in a wok or pan and lightly fry onion. Add nettles, peas, sweet potato, salt and pepper. Mix then serve hot.

Spagnetti
6 handfuls nettles
spaghetti
1 chopped onion
1 crushed clove garlic
1 chilli
1 pint good vegetable stock
Olive oil

Simmer nettles in boiling water for a few minutes. In a separate saucepan heat a little olive oil, stir in onion, garlic and chilli. Simmer until tender then add vegetable stock and nettles. Cook the spaghetti in water then drain off water. Drain the nettle mixture, add the spaghetti then serve.

Nettled pasta
250g nettles
450g pasta
225g ricotta cheese
175ml olive oil
2 tbsps parsley cut
2 tbsps mint cut
2 tbsps chives cut
Juice and rind of 1 lemon
Pinch of salt, pepper

Bring pasta to the boil and while it is simmering bring nettles to the boil and simmer 5 minutes. Drain nettles. Put in processor and mix for 1 minute. Slowly add oil and process to a puree. Add cheese, lemon juice, rind, parsley, mint, chives. Salt, pepper. Blend. Drain pasta and retain 1mugful of the water. Stir nettle mix into pasta. Slowly add as much of the retained mugful of water as necessary to make a smooth sauce. Serve.

Nettled risotto
160g nettles
950ml chicken or vegetable stock
175g cooked peas
350g risotto rice
2 garlic cloves, crushed
1 chopped onion
4 tablespoons olive oil
150ml white wine
80g cheese, grated
salt and pepper

In a saucepan warm two tablespoon of the olive oil. Stir in nettles, peas and simmer 5 minutes. Add 60ml of the stock puree and leave to one side. In a saucepan warm remaining olive oil, add garlic, onion, salt, pepper and simmer until soft. Add rice, wine and remaining stock. Boil, cover and cook for 30 minutes in an oven pre-heated to 190c. Add the nettle puree then serve with the cheese sprinkled on top.

Waterless steamed nettles
Waterless steamed nettles are quite delicious. Put a little boiling water in a saucepan then put the nettles in a colander on top of the saucepan, put a lid on top and let the steam do the cooking. You will be pleasantly surprised with the result.

Waterless nettles
Put nettles, a knob of butter and a little salt in a saucepan. Keep turning and simmering for 15 minutes. Add a pinch of nutmeg, pepper and a knob of butter then serve.

Nettleade
2 kg nettle leaves
white sugar
4 litres water
slices of lemon

In a saucepan bring nettles and water to near boiling. Simmer for 50 minutes. Discard nettles (to compost). Measure water and return water to saucepan. For every 200 ml water stir in 160g sugar. Simmer for 45 minutes until thick. Cool then dilute with water and serve with lime, lemon or orange slices.

Although the Irish have a saying that 'there's no cold like the cold in the Spring ' some folk do enjoy the following:

Cold nettled soup
1 lb – 500g – nettles finely chopped
Knob butter
Some finely chopped onion, cucumber, green pepper, tomatoes, chives
Sour cream
Some herbs such as dill, basil, angelica or marjoram
Salt, cold water, lemon juice.

Put nettles and butter in a saucepan and sauté for 5 minutes. Mix in cold water, onion, dill, basil, angelica, marjoram. Bring to the boil and simmer 15 minutes. Allow to cool. Add sour cream, cucumber, green pepper, tomatoes, salt, lemon juice. Sprinkle chives on top, chill in fridge then serve.

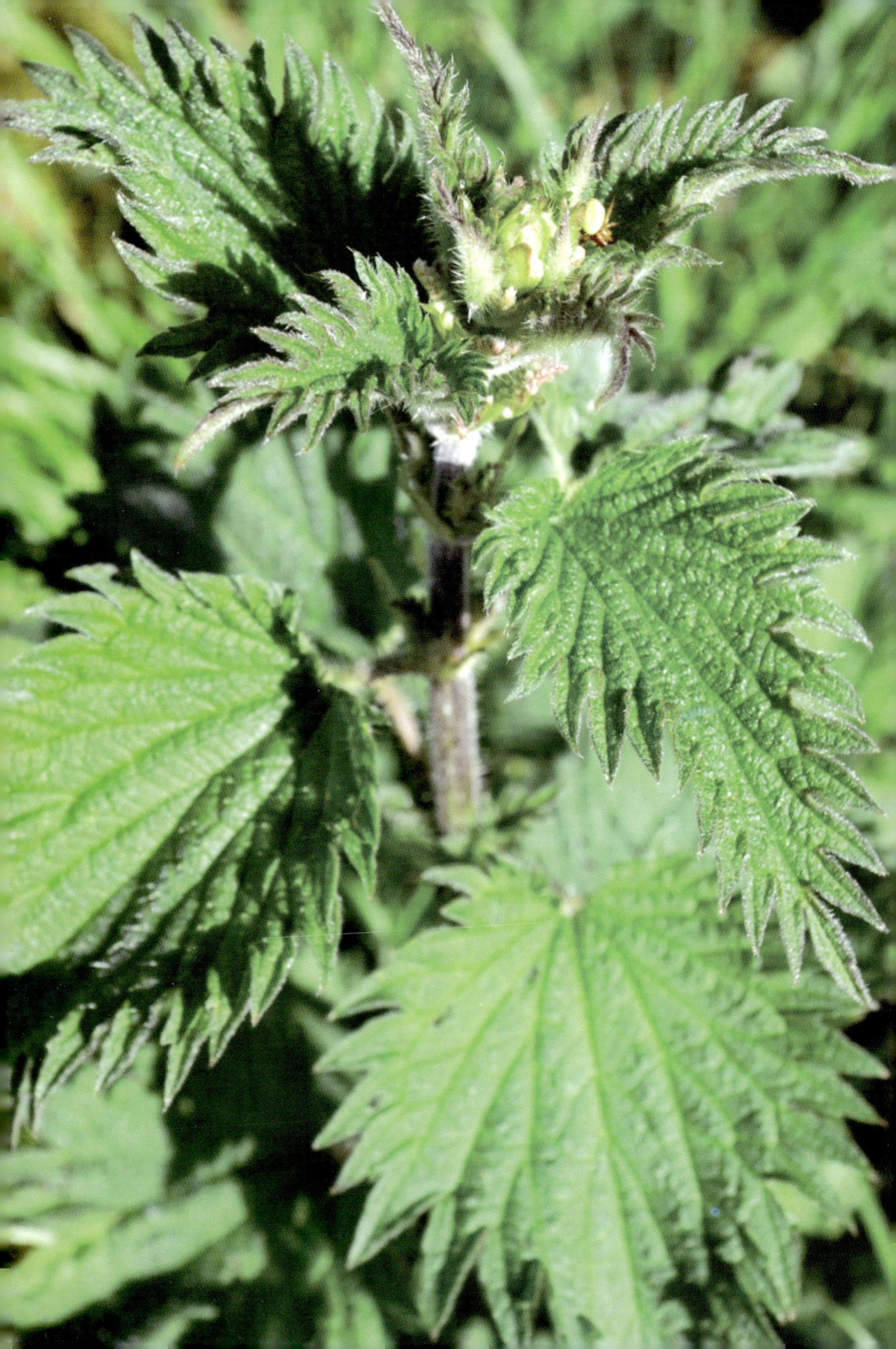

CHAPTER SEVEN

The feel good factor

The Romans had an extensive knowledge of herbs. The famous Botanist Dr Dioscorides Pedanios occasionally travelled with the Roman troops. Years later when the Roman soldiers arrived to invade Britain they were probably aware that nettles already grew in the cold British climate, yet they brought their essential, precious nettle and nettle-seeds with them. The soldiers relied on nettles for whole body strength and they also rubbed their limbs with nettles to numb them against the cold. The Romans were responsible for the initial introduction of around 200 herbs to Britain, including the Roman nettles *(Urtica pilulifera)* which, although rare, still grows today, mainly beside the seaside, around the east of England.

Nettles are an indication as to the whereabouts of ancient human settlements as they grow near people, where they thrive and flourish on arable, fertile humus soil enriched with animals and people's waste. Wherever you see a big bed of nettles, be assured there is healthy soil underneath.

In Salisbury, England, villages which have been derelict for almost 1,600 years, still have nettles thriving among the underground rubble.

Nettles also grow near the underground tunnels which lead to the homes of elves and Earth-fairies.

Irish mythology tells us that Oisin was the son of Fionn mac Cumhaill and leader of the Fianna. After 300 years he returned to the hill of Almhuin, which is now the parish of Allen in Co Kildare and found nothing except grass and nettles. Oisin is reputed to be buried in Cushendall, Co Antrim.

Also after centuries in exile, the Children of Lir returned home to find it derelict except for grass and bunches of nettles.

It is common knowledge throughout the whole of Ireland that if one finds comfrey and nettle growing together it is certain that a monastery once stood on that site.

Years ago in Ireland a woman was receiving the Holy Communion host during Mass when it slipped from her mouth and fell down a hole in the floor. Eventually the Church building collapsed but a bunch of nettles grew protectively over the spot where the host lay. A priest and a local labourer searched the nettles and found the host safe and sound.

Apparently Saint Brigid once had a lot of folk arrive when her cupboard was bare so she miraculously transformed tree bark into food and nettles into butter for her visitors to dine on. Folklore tells us that St Colmcille insisted on fasting during the whole of Lent while eating nothing except nettles, water and salt gruel. His cook was worried about him but St Colmcille maintained he would eat only what came from the pot-stick, so the cook added oatmeal and milk to the gruel then altered the pot-stick so the gruel travelled down it. Being a man of his word, St Colmcille did eat the altered gruel.

During the Irish famine many folk stayed alive by eating nettles, seaweed (carrageen) and field mustard (charlock).

Years ago in Ireland the Irish meal Colcannon (cal ceannfhionn) was made with nettles although nowadays cabbage or kale is used instead. In Co Leitrim, nettle bruisy was called 'sods of turf' and it was made by mashing together nettles, boiled potatoes and butter then cutting into little squares.

On May eve (April 30th) in southern Cork, it was customary to hold 'nettlemas night' (Feile na Neantog) where boys and girls danced outside holding bunches of nettles and stinging each other. The Anglo-Saxons included powdered nettle in their 'Nine Herbs Charm' to cure infections.

Long ago in Wales an old pagan custom was to leave a small undisturbed bunch of nettles growing in the garden as an offering to the devil. This could have originated from the Welsh myth about the maiden Blodeuedd who was created out of flowers, one of which was the nettle flower. Blodeuedd had a fiery temper and her stinging words could have cut you to the bone.

Samuel Pepys (1661) ate and quite enjoyed nettle porridge. In Devon and Cornwall, May 1st was traditionally called 'stinging nettle day'.

The English used to have a 'be nice to nettles week' held during May each year, while, up until recently, Dorset annually hosted the world nettle eating championship which originated in 1986 when two farmers argued over whose field grew the tallest nettle.

In Turkey nettle is regularly added to spring dishes with nettle and spinach pie being a popular favourite.
In California acres of nettles are being cultivated for their culinary and healing properties, while the wise Californian gardeners understand how butterflies are attracted to nettles.

In Scotland nettle was a common ingredient in porridge and soup. Gardeners cultivated nettles underneath hand-glasses which were then eaten as 'early spring kale'. The Scots made the nettle pudding haggis inside the stomach of a sheep. The Irish version of haggis is *proinnseach* and a muslin bag is used instead of a sheep's stomach.

Wet a handful of nettles and simmer for five minutes. Strain, add butter, sea salt, black pepper, onion and simmer a further five minutes until a puree. Lightly cook a cupful of oatmeal (or rice) and fry a few rashers of bacon. Mix oatmeal and bacon into the nettle puree along with some cabbage and two leeks. Secure mixture in a muslin bag, boil for one hour, then serve with gravy or melted butter.

When nettles are boiled in water with a large amount of salt the resulting liquid can be used as a substitute for rennet in cheese making.

Oul country saying:
Nettles in March,
Muggons (Mugwort – Artemisia vulgaris) – in May,
Would have many a one living,
That's laid in the clay.

In Ireland, you'll notice that a lot of small old houses have their front door just touching the roadside. I used to wonder how the owners avoided being hit by passing traffic as they stood chatting to the people. But, of course, years ago there wasn't much traffic and I think the doors were intentionally situated next to the roadside to enable passers-by to feel welcome to call on their ceili.

Although our home place is off the roadside we had a lot of ceiliers. My deep love of folklore began as I listened to these yarns of ghosts, banshees, sceachs and fairies or the gentry as some call them.

During one of those evenings a relative recited the ancient superstition to get rid of a fever. Pull a nettle, including the roots, out of the ground and as you do so, keep repeating the name of the ailing person and also, the names of the ailing person's mother or father.

A Welsh custom is to put a bunch of nettles under the pillow of an ailing person. If the nettles remain green the ailing person will survive, but if the nettles lose their colour the ailing person will die.

My father used to maintain "say nothing but play away at the thinking" referred to the 'unspoken', an old Scottish custom that nettles had to be gathered at midnight and nobody was to speak to the person as they gathered the nettles or the healing power of the nettles would be lessened.

Relatives of my husband, on holidays from England, told us of an unusual 'cure' for 'bad' eyes, which they heard about, while in Devonshire: If a girl has 'bad' eyes a 'cure' can be obtained by going each morning, for nine consecutive mornings, to a man who has never laid eyes on his mother. The man holds up a nettle leaf, which has a little hole in it, and blows into the girl's eyes, through the hole. The man must perform this action, early in the morning, before he has done any chore of any kind. If a boy has 'bad' eyes, he must go to a woman who has never laid eyes on her father, to obtain this 'cure'.

I once heard my uncle say 'the devil is good to his own'". He was referring to a bandit in a TV western who had got off, again, with some sneaky deed and my uncle was insinuating that like will not harm like.

There is an old saying 'the nettle will never be struck down by lightning.' The Irish believe that if you carry a few nettles in your pocket lightning will not strike you and that growing nettles near your home or outhouses gives protection from lightning. Interestingly, houseleek – *sempervivum* – whose nickname is thunder plant, is grown on walls for the same protection.

In some counties in Ireland it is believed that your home will be protected from lightning all year if a hawthorn branch is broken (not cut) off and put inside the home on Ascension Thursday only. Every other day, it is bad luck to bring hawthorn flowers into the house.

Some people tie bunches of nettles to broomsticks in their gardens to scare birds.

Growing nettles nearby will deter flies and also prevent any milk in the house from being curdled by witches, wizards and house trolls. Although nettles were used against witchcraft, witches used nettles in their witchcraft.

For swellings, a herb woman (bean na luibheanna) called Biddy Early applied a poultice of nettles, watercress and cabbage leaf all set with egg white, while it is reputed that a poultice made from boiled nettles applied to haemorrhoids will ease the discomfort.

Develop your own nettle plot
Earlier we discussed how vital a role nettles play in the survival of our fascinating wildlife. If you want to attract some of our astonishingly beautiful butterflies, of which we have approximately thirty three species (plus around two thousand moths) in Ireland, pick as big a patch as you can spare in a sunny but sheltered site. No doubt the whole neighbourhood will be queuing to give you their nettles, but before you plant them approximately 3ft (90cm) apart add plenty of manure or compost or your own nettle liquid fertiliser (how to make fertiliser is explained next) to the soil as nettles are quite greedy plants.

Note that herbs or vegetables thrive better when grown beside nettles. Nettles planted alongside brassicas and legumes will lure cabbage white butterflies and aphids. Angelica oil will increase when planted alongside nettles. Remember that perennial nettles will self seed and underground their strong stems (even if broken) can grow up to almost 36 inches annually.

Nettle Compost Activator
As nettles are rich in nitrogen they are ideal for cutting all year round, even out of season, and adding to the compost heap as an activator along with yarrow leaves (woundwort), Achillea millefolium and comfrey leaves (knitbone) Symphytum officinale. Wear gloves when handling comfrey as it can irritate skin.

Nettle liquid fertiliser
You can also make your own free nettle liquid fertiliser.
Have ready an old barrel or tub which has no leak holes in it. Gather as many nettles as will almost fill the barrel.

First, crunch the nettles by running the lawn mower over them or else use your thickly gloved hands. Put the nettles into the barrel, then put on the top of the nettles a couple of old wire cooling trays or a bit of wire mesh.

On top of this put a heavy stone or block. Add water to almost fill the barrel.
Your fertiliser should be ready in about one month and can be diluted
1 part fertiliser to approximately 8 – 10 parts water. This fertiliser smells nasty so best to keep it away from your back door. Secure mesh wire on top so air can circulate and be EXTRA SURE that the wire mesh can NOT be removed by children.

Your plants, tomatoes, herbs and nettles will thrive on this! Keep adding more nettles and water all year round. One woman told me that when she frequently sprays her plants with this chemical-free nettle fertiliser (using rainwater) she has no problems with pests and it deters blackfly on broad beans (Both summer savory – *satureia hortensis* –

and dill – *anethum graveolens* – grown beside broad beans will help deter blackfly).

Another gentleman I know uses this fertiliser on his beloved roses yet he just waters the soil around the rose roots. My husband John sprays this liquid onto our growing potato tops to discourage blight and so far so good.

Chlorophyll is the substance that makes our precious plants green and which assists in the production of oxygen, so that we inhale whatever trees and plants exhale. Chlorophyll is also a natural deodorant and nettles have lots of it, which is why nettle infusion makes a truly great mouth wash.

CHAPTER EIGHT

For health and beauty

Nettle spa
If you suffer from pains or if you just want to experience one of the most refreshing baths of your life, try the following which has to be experienced to be believed.
Unlike some bubble baths which leave your skin feeling caked and dry, a nettle bath will leave your skin squeaky clean yet rejuvenated.

Almost fill a carrier bag with stinging nettle leaves, stems and also roots. As they are for bathing it doesn't matter if they're out-of-season.

Put all in a large saucepan, cover with cold water and leave to steep overnight. Next day slowly bring to the boil, leave to simmer 30 minutes then lift nettles out and add liquid to bath water. Do not use any bubble bath or soap – just lie and relax for about 30 minutes in pure natural bliss.

Another quicker, yet highly effective, variation on above is to just put the bagful of stinging nettle leaves, stems and roots, (roots are optional) directly into the bath. Run enough hot water to quarter-fill the bath and leave to steep for approximately 30 minutes. Then fill the bath with water. Remove the nettles with gloved hands, as they can still sting. Some folk intentionally leave a few nettles in the bath water and hope that the stings will ease their pains. Again, add no bubble bath or soap then just lie back and experience half an hour in heaven on earth.

Nettle foot spa
Gather a few handfuls of stinging nettles, stems and include roots, if possible. Put in a saucepan, cover with cold water and leave to steep overnight.

Next day bring just to the boil, simmer for about 10 minutes, strain nettles and add liquid to the water in your foot-spa. Do not add any soap or bubble bath though a spoonful of dried mustard powder is beneficial. Immerse your exhausted feet for about 15 minutes and your poor soles will feel fresh and rejuvenated.

Nettles for your scalp and hair
An excellent tonic for thin, falling, lack-lustre hair is to massage a little nettle tea into your scalp daily or make an infusion of stinging nettle leaves and roots then massage a little into the scalp daily. To combat dandruff comb nettle tea through the hair before massaging the scalp daily. Another remedy for dull, lifeless hair is a tincture I learned about years ago. This remedy includes alcohol but I am including it in this section as it is for EXTERNAL use only.

Nettle hair tincture
Dig up, wipe with a cloth (or disused soft nailbrush) and slice enough nettle roots to almost fill a (preferably brown or green) glass jar or bottle. Pour over and cover the roots with either Poitin (illegally distilled Irish whisky) or vodka or rye whisky (38-40% strength) then leave sealed jar to sit in a warm room for at least two weeks, shaking regularly. Strain and massage a little tincture into scalp daily. Don't forget to add the residue to your compost heap. You can preserve this tincture in the fridge if you wish. Just when we're mentioning hair, did you know that another excellent remedy for falling hair is to massage a little infusion of Southernwood *(artemisia abrotanum)* into the scalp daily. This is a beautiful aromatic herb, which is nicknamed lad's love, that I grow in pots, just outside our door so we can brush against it and enjoy its heavenly scent.

Nettle steam facial
Cleansing nettles are great for getting rid of impurities. Put a good handful of nettles in a bowl then fill the bowl with boiling water. Cover your head and the bowl with a towel for 20 minutes then rinse your face in cool water.

Urtication
The ancient Russian tradition of urtication which dates back approximately 2,000 years is still used today as a country remedy for frozen shoulder, lumbago, rheumatism and sciatica.

Sciatica
Using freshly gathered stinging nettles begin at your foot and gently brush upwards on the outside of your leg then gently brush downwards on the inside of your leg, ending at your foot. Follow by gently brushing right across your hips thus producing a prickling sensation then a tingling heat which stimulates and tones weak nerves, wasted muscles and poor circulation.

Do use caution and go very gently with this remedy as some people experience shock when stung by nettles. If you wish, you can crush the nettles first, then rub the crumpled, powdered bits on the affected parts.

Bleeding
During the Second World War, finely crushed dried nettle leaves were used to dress wounds and hasten healing.

To stop a minor cut bleeding, either apply crushed, dried nettles or a few crushed yarrow leaves or cover with a cobweb or sprinkle on a little cayenne pepper. Cayenne will sting but it does a good job.

Nowadays German researchers are working with a mixture of nettle root extract and saw palmetto for benign prostatic hyperplasia (BPH).

Nettles and livestock

My mother maintained that poultry, especially turkeys, will thrive and fatten-up if sliced nettles are added to its meal and chickens will increase their egg production.
Asses gobble up nettles mixed in with their food. Dried nettles can be made into bales of hay then fed to milking cattle to increase their milk flow while nettle hay fed to horses and goats will soon make their coats thicker and shinier. Pigs can be lured to eat boiled nettles if they are mixed into their yellowmeal.

Nettle fibre

The net in nettle is to spin and for centuries yarns made from nettle fibres have been spun and woven into different types of durable fine and coarse cloth such as table cloths, sheets, sailcloth, anchor ropes and even parachutes. In Scandinavia, during the 18th century nettles were grown for their fibre and culinary use, while Thomas Campbell, the Scottish poet wrote about tablecloths and sheets derived from nettles.

During the First World War nettles were used to substitute cotton. The German army wore uniforms made from nettle fibre mixed with Ramie (Boehmeria nivea). Ramie is nettle's tropical relative used in the manufacture of gas masks, during the War.

During the Second World War the chlorophyll in nettles was extracted to make permanent green dye for military uniforms and nets.

Boiled nettle roots will produce a lovely yellow dye widely used in Russia. Native Americans included strong, smooth, fibrous nettle stems in craft-making while in parts of Europe the stems have been used in paper making.

Nettles call
Hopefully our Urticaceae family's environmentally friendly nettle will help to alleviate our worldwide paper shortage. Think of all the wonderful trees whose lives could be saved and nettles are certainly not difficult to cultivate. I feel annoyed that we are surrounded by so many strong, valuable and exhilarating nettles which are wasted and lost. I am convinced these unsung heroes could be beneficial to the health and wellbeing of our precious loved ones, our vitally important environment and ourselves because when we feel good we are better people and when we are better people our whole world is a much better place.

Our wonderfully-gifted stinging nettle is a healer, a survivor, a quare good plant – and sure its only natural.

Marian Conway
Green Gate Farm

Marian Conway lives with her husband John and their three children in South Derry, three miles from Lough Neagh, the largest freshwater lake in Ireland and the British Isles. Marian is a former sub-postmistress and her passions are exploring Ireland, meeting people and nature but her obsession is gardening, especially growing her own food.